# ROSIEVILLE

MARY RACHEL BROWN

**CURRENCY PRESS**
The performing arts publisher

CANBERRA
YOUTH THEATRE

CURRENT THEATRE SERIES

First published in 2023
by Currency Press
Gadigal Land, Suite 310, 46-56 Kippax Street, Surry Hills NSW 2010 Australia
enquiries@currency.com.au
www.currency.com.au

in association with Canberra Youth Theatre

Typeset by Brighton Gray for Currency Press.
Cover background image by Adam McGrath.
Front cover shows Imogen Bigsby-Chamberlion.
Cover design by Luke Rogers.

Currency Press acknowledges the Traditional Owners of the Country on which we live and work. We pay our respects to all Aboriginal and Torres Strait Islander Elders, past and present.

NATIONAL
LIBRARY
OF AUSTRALIA

A catalogue record for this book is available from the National Library of Australia

# Contents

*For Ken*

*Rosieville* was first produced by Canberra Youth Theatre at The Courtyard Studio, Canberra Theatre Centre, Ngunnawal Land on 29 September 2023, with the following cast:

| | |
|---|---|
| ROSE | Imogen Bigsby-Chamberlin |
| XAVIER | Oscar Abraham |
| LIZ | Amy Crawford |
| ALAN | Richard Manning |
| ANIKA | Disa Swifte |
| BEN | Callum Doherty |
| PIGEON / CINDY | Clare Imlach |

Director, Luke Rogers
Set and Costume Designer, Aislinn King
Lighting Designer, Ethan Hamill
Sound Designer and Composer, Patrick Haesler
Assistant Director, Emily Austin
Stage Manager, Rhiley Winnett
Assistant Stage Manager, Hannah McGinness

## CHARACTERS

Welcome to Button Place!

**Number 1 Button Place**
ROSE OLYMPIA LIVINGSTON, 11
XAVIER LIVINGSTONE, 14
LIZ LIVINGSTONE, 37, Rose and Xavier's mum

**Number 3 Button Place**
ALAN SAYED, 64
ANIKA SAYED, 18, Alan's daughter and carer

**Number 4 Button Place**
BEN SPITERI, 17, Anika's boyfriend

**Déjà Do Hair Salon**
CINDY, 20

**Dream World**
PIGEON, ageless

**The Birdman Rally**
COMMENTATOR, a shock-jock-type voiceover

## NOTES

Cindy and Pigeon are to be played by the same actor.

The author encourages casting that reflects the diversity in Australian society.

This play text went to press before the end of rehearsals and may differ from the play as performed.

## SCENE ONE—DREAM WORLD

*Rose's bedroom—night.*

*A messy bed is covered in toys, cushions, books and clothes. It is impossible to tell if there is anyone sleeping under this endless amount of stuff.*

*A sudden clap of thunder cuts through the silence. A shower of feathers rains down from above.*

ROSE *sits bolt upright.*

PIGEON *emerges, they are wearing a helmet which has a flashlight attached.* ROSE *is caught like a bunny in the headlight.*

ROSE: Every night, at the same time—
PIGEON: I'm punctual—
ROSE: A pigeon crash-lands in my room.
PIGEON: Because you're my job—
ROSE: At first, I think it's dead—
PIGEON: Just a rough landing—
ROSE: Then it starts talking.
PIGEON: I'm your subconscious.
ROSE: What?
PIGEON: I'm in charge of your dreams. Why are you looking at me like that?
ROSE: I just expected my subconscious to be …
PIGEON: Spill?
ROSE: … A little less lame.
PIGEON: Wow! Rude! Some people get cockroaches or maggots. How would you feel if your spirit animal was a maggot? It happens, so count yourself lucky you got me. Us pigeons are the real deal, we know both the ground and the sky, and we're not afraid of dirt and mess. We can handle mega jobs like you.
ROSE: I'm not a mega job.
PIGEON: Yeah, you are. You're a hot mess, lady!
ROSE: Calm your farm.
PIGEON: You are dangerously close to tipping this conversation into nightmare territory. Is that what you want?

ROSE: No, I just want to have a regular dream with stuff like talking backwards underwater and flying—flying shouldn't be a stretch for you.

PIGEON: You can't fly away from what is coming. See tomorrow, rude girl!

> PIGEON *takes off, they miss the window, hit the wall, and fall to the ground.*
>
> *Silence.*

ROSE: … Are you alright?

> *Beat.* PIGEON *speaks whilst still on ground recovering from their crash-landing.*

PIGEON: Do you know what heartbreak is, Rose?

ROSE: Do I need to?

PIGEON: Yep.

ROSE: Why?

PIGEON: Look into my eyes.

ROSE: Can you turn your headlight off?

PIGEON: No!

ROSE: It's hurting my eyes.

PIGEON: This is going to hurt, Rose.

ROSE: What do you mean by that?

PIGEON: See you tomorrow.

ROSE: Wait—

> PIGEON *takes off, they miss the window, hit the wall, and fall to the ground again.*

PIGEON: Why? Why is there a wall there? Why!

ROSE: This is a bedroom, it has walls.

PIGEON: Don't get smart!

ROSE: Do you need a hand?

> PIGEON *makes a show of getting up.*

PIGEON: No, take this in, take a good look, this is struggle, this is damage, this suffering, this is hardship, this is getting knocked down and getting back up again, this is—

ROSE: Okay, I got it.

PIGEON: I don't think you do.

> PIGEON *zigzags then struggles to get out of the window.*

ROSE: Are you okay?

PIGEON: We are not okay, Rose. That is why I'm here. We got shit to sort out. Strap yourself in. You're about to wake up big time.

> PIGEON *disappears through the window then doubles back.*

Warning. Incoming.

## SCENE TWO—BORDER CONTROL

*Rose's bedroom—morning.*

LIZ, *Rose's mother, enters and opens the curtains.*

LIZ: Good morning.

ROSE: No.

LIZ: … Rose?

ROSE: I'm asleep—

LIZ: Come on, rise and shine.

ROSE: Don't ask me to shine.

LIZ: Just rise then.

ROSE: I'm tired.

LIZ: From sleeping ten hours?

ROSE: I have a very active dream life.

LIZ: What about having an active real life and cleaning this room?

> LIZ *hops on the bed.*

What's this?

> LIZ *removes the feather from* ROSE's *hair.*

ROSE: Give it to me—

LIZ: I don't mind you spending time with Anika and the pigeons, but you have to wash your hair, Rose.

ROSE: I did but then I had a dream about a pigeon, so—

LIZ: So? You dreamt this feather into your hair?

ROSE: I'll wash it tonight.

LIZ: Or we could book in for a wash, cut and blow-dry!

ROSE: No.

LIZ: Come on, we could both use a little pick-me-up.

ROSE: No—

LIZ: Why not?

ROSE: The name of the place for starters. Who calls a hair salon Déjà Do?

LIZ: I challenge you to come up with a better name.

ROSE: How about 'I'll Cut You'.

LIZ: Rose!

ROSE: 'Curl Up and Dye'.

LIZ: I really don't know what part of your brain comes up with this stuff.

ROSE: Yes you do.

*Beat.*

Going to Déjà Do feels like losing.

LIZ *is taken aback.*

LIZ: What do you mean by that?

ROSE: Remember last time we went?

LIZ: I'm not going to do anything crazy this time. I just want a little trim. Your brother could do with a cut as well. We could make it a family—

ROSE: Count me out.

*Beat.* LIZ *gives the feather back to* ROSE.

LIZ: What's wrong Rosie?

ROSE: Nothing.

LIZ: Really?

*Beat.*

Because if you are counting your way from one day to the next again—

ROSE: I don't do that anymore, Mum.

LIZ: Okay but you tell me if it starts up again, deal?

ROSE: Yeah, yeah.

*Beat.*

LIZ: Permission to cross the border, officer?

ROSE: What? No—

LIZ: Please, officer, you have to let me into Rosieville, my daughter's there and we haven't talked properly in ages.

ROSE: Please don't—

LIZ: Come on, officer, I haven't got all day. Let me in!

ROSE: Mum?

*LIZ gets a card out from her wallet.*

LIZ: Come on, here's my passport, officer.

ROSE: That's a library card, Mum.

*LIZ presents another card.*

LIZ: Sorry, officer—

ROSE: Dan Murphy's rewards card—

LIZ: Yes, but you pretend it's my passport, you remember how to play.

ROSE: From when I was seven years old!

LIZ: I want to speak to your supervisor!

ROSE: Technically, that's you, Mum.

LIZ: LET ME INTO ROSIEVILLE NOW, OR I WILL TRASH THIS ENTIRE ESTABLISHMENT—

*LIZ starts throwing things off Rose's bed.*

ROSE: Stop it, Mum! Please.

*Beat.*

LIZ: So we have outgrown going to Rosieville, have we?

ROSE: Yes, I have!

LIZ: You should never outgrow telling people how you feel.

ROSE: Spare me the TED Talk.

LIZ: … Rose—

ROSE: What's the point of going to a place where I tell you everything when you can't tell me the one thing I want to know.

*Pause. LIZ strokes Rose's hair.*

LIZ: If I knew when your dad was going to come back, I'd tell you, okay?

*Beat.*

Come on, up. And no visiting Anika on the way to school, you'll be late.

*LIZ gets off the bed, ready to exit.*

ROSE: Don't go to Déjà Do. It never helps. You always end up looking sad and weird for weeks until whatever mistake you've made grows out. Just leave your hair like it is.

LIZ *sits back down on the bed, facing away from* ROSE.

LIZ: Rosie, I'd never wash my hair again and let it grow down to my ankles if I thought it would make a difference, I really would. I'm ... I am ... sorry, I know this is hard.

ROSE: ... Mum?

LIZ: I'm fine.

ROSE: Mum!—

LIZ: Just give me a minute.

ROSE: It's just you're sitting on my leg.

LIZ *moves.*

LIZ: Sorry.

*Beat.*

Come on, you're going to be late. Chop chop!

## *SCENE THREE—BIRDMAN*

*The shed.*

XAVIER *is asleep in a sleeping bag.* ALAN *enters, startling* XAVIER, ALAN *in turn gets startled by* XAVIER. *They both scream.*

XAVIER: Alan, you can't just walk in, this is my shed.

ALAN: I'm your neighbour.

XAVIER: Doesn't mean you can break and enter.

ALAN: Have you been sleeping out here since your dad left?

XAVIER: None of your business.

ALAN: Is it helping?

*Pause.*

Xavier, there are two types of tiger in this world—

XAVIER: Here we go—

ALAN: Do you remember what they are?

XAVIER: The tiger that lives in the jungle, and the tiger that lives in the zoo. I really don't need this speech right now—

ALAN: Most people end up being zoo tigers.

XAVIER: Yeah, yeah—

ALAN: Most of them don't even know what put them in the cage, some—

XAVIER *and* ALAN: Don't even realise they're in a cage.

ALAN: That's right, and—

XAVIER: What do you want Alan?

ALAN: Where is it?

XAVIER: What?

ALAN: You're going round telling everybody in the street you're in here building a flying machine. So where is it?

XAVIER: I'm not doing it anymore.

ALAN: Why?

XAVIER: No-one ever flew at the Birdman Rally. I googled it. It's just people in stupid costumes jumping off a platform and falling head-first into the lake. The whole thing was and is a classic case of misguided community spirit.

ALAN: Totally agree. Back in the day, the majority of Birdman entrants were half-inebriated, half-naked, attention-seeking fully grown dickheads attempting to fly with zero preparation! Shameful … that's just what the eighties were like, it was a reckless era.

XAVIER: So why bring it back it?

ALAN: Because some of us actually flew. George Reekie flew fifty metres in ninety-one.

XAVIER: Who cares?

ALAN: I do, I was runner-up, I never really been able to come to terms with being beaten by Reekie, I'm haunted by it actually.

XAVIER: Not my problem.

*Beat.*

ALAN: So, you're just going to sit out here on your own viping—

XAVIER: Vaping—

ALAN: Looking at that phone, and drinking can after can of this crap?

XAVIER: We were going to build the wings out of Red Bull cans. Dad's idea.

*Beat.*

ALAN: Xavier, I think you'd feel better if you did something.

XAVIER: Like jumping off a platform and falling—

ALAN: Flying—

XAVIER: Falling—
ALAN: Flying—
XAVIER: Falling. I don't want to fall.
ALAN: Everyone ends up falling, even the winner. Come on—
XAVIER: No. I don't want to fall head-first into a shit-coloured lake and humiliate myself for other people's entertainment. I've made up my mind, not doing it.
ALAN: I could help you build—
XAVIER: No!
ALAN: So you're saying no to my forty-plus years of aeronautical experience?
XAVIER: I would not call pigeon-fancying aeronautical experience, Alan.

> *Pause.*

ALAN: Set me up one of those vapes will you?
XAVIER: … What?
ALAN: I'm bored! You don't want my help, I'm looking to fill the void. So … hook a brother up.
XAVIER: What?
ALAN: Hook a brother up with a vape.
XAVIER: You shouldn't vape.
ALAN: Must be expensive? You know you get fifty grand if you win the Birdman?
XAVIER: If you fly over fifty metres, like that is ever going to happen.
ALAN: I flew forty-eight-point-seven in eighty-six. Come on, Xavier, you don't get many chances to beat the odds, and this is one, let's build a flying machine!
XAVIER: I told everyone that I was building it with my dad.
ALAN: So, say you built it with your dad. Whatever gets you through, and it works for me, I don't want people knowing I have a spare fifty grand under my pillow.
XAVIER: Alan, if we won, we would split the money.
ALAN: Deal. Let's start with the wings and work our way into the harness.
XAVIER: No.
ALAN: Alright, you're forcing my hand, set me up a vape. You leave me with no alternative but to vape the rest of my short life away.
XAVIER: Alan—

ALAN: Who can say if it will be the vaping or the boredom that finally kills me, but either way, I'll blame you.

XAVIER: Oh, give it a break—

ALAN: Pushing drugs on a sick, vulnerable old man. You should be ashamed of yourself! And don't think I won't tell your mother you got me hooked on the vaping.

XAVIER: What?

ALAN: Liz!

XAVIER: No!

ALAN: Liz!

XAVIER: Shhhh, Jesus!

ALAN: Your son's running a drug den out here!

XAVIER: Alan!

ALAN: He's got his pimps onto me, and he—

XAVIER: Shut up!

ALAN: Alright, calm down!

XAVIER: You calm down!

ALAN: I AM CALM! CALM AS ALL HELL!

> *Pause.*

XAVIER: … Pimps?

ALAN: You have to understand, you are dealing with a jungle tiger here, Xav, so I suggest you agree with me. Here's the deal, I won't tell your mum you're a drug lord—

XAVIER: Oh my God—

ALAN: If you let me help you build a flying machine?

XAVIER: That's blackmail.

ALAN: Correct. So, what's it going to be tiger? Zoo or jungle?

XAVIER: … Do I have to—

ALAN: Liz, your boy has gone wick-wack in his tic-tac, he is going to pop a cap in my melon Helen if I download with the upload—

XAVIER: What?

ALAN: I know how drug lords talk. Zoo or Jungle?

> *Beat.*

> Liz—

XAVIER: Alright! … Wings first you reckon?

ALAN: Yes! We work out what we need to carry you—the wings, then we work out what we need to keep you safe—the harness.

ANIKA *enters in a panic.*

ANIKA: Dad!

ALAN: Yes—

ANIKA: I was worried sick.

ALAN: So you should be. You're my carer, and you go and lose me!

ANIKA: Well, if you had of let me know where you were going!

ALAN: Not my job to tell you where I'm going. I might not even know where I'm going.

ANIKA: Well, you can't just take off.

ALAN: I can and I did. How on earth could you be so careless, I am a big unit, it is not as though I am easy to lose. This is your last warning, lose me again and I'll have no choice but to cut you out of my will.

ANIKA: I'm your daughter.

ALAN: Don't play the daughter card with me. I'm just laying out your work conditions, which include subcontracting you to Xavier every morning and afternoon to help build a flying machine.

ANIKA: A what?

ALAN: A flying machine?

XAVIER: We are entering the Birdman Rally.

ANIKA: Just the combination of the words 'bird' and 'man' unsettles me.

XAVIER: If you can fly fifty metres over the lake you win fifty grand.

ANIKA: What!

ALAN: You're just a subcontractor, the money will be split between Xavier and I.

XAVIER: If Anika helps we'll split it three ways—

ALAN: Over my dead body!

XAVIER: My shed my rules.

ANIKA: Where do you want me to start, boss?

XAVIER: Ummmm, well all these cans have to be flattened, before we can do anything with them.

ANIKA *abruptly stamps on a can of Red Bull. Beat. She stamps on another, then another and another. Every can stamp releasing her frustration.*

ALAN: [*to* XAVIER] Well, don't just stand there, it's not as though you haven't got anything to get out of your system.

XAVIER *looks resistant but joins* ANIKA *in stamping on cans. Eventually, he too is taken over by the can-crushing satisfaction.* ANIKA *lets out a scream of determination,* XAVIER *joins her.*

That's the spirit!

*Once every can is flattened, both* XAVIER *and* ANIKA *are breathless.*

How does it feel to be back in the land of the living?

ANIKA: Surprisingly good.

ALAN: Wasn't asking you! Xavier?

XAVIER: Work in progress.

ALAN *holds his hand to his stomach.*

ANIKA: You alright, Dad?

ALAN: We'll get back to this after my racing pigeon comes in tomorrow arvo.

XAVIER: No rush.

ANIKA: Come on, Dad, let's go.

ALAN: I want you both there to see my girl come home, it will teach you a thing or two about landing in the right place.

*SCENE FOUR—WAITING*

*Alan's backyard.*

*Enter* ANIKA. *We hear the sound of pigeons cooing and wings flapping.*

*The presence of the pigeons is represented by the actors' gaze and the belief they imbue.*

ANIKA *hands* ROSE *some birdseed, they feed the pigeons.*

ROSE: Do you ever look at them and wish you were one of them?

ANIKA: If I was one of them, I wouldn't get to be the human who looks after them.

*Beat.*

Do you wish you were one of them?

ROSE: Yeah, I like the way they can fly above everything and see what's coming.

ANIKA: Make sure Greta Thunberg and Ruth Ginsburg get some—

ROSE: How do you know which one is which?

ANIKA: You love them. When I first started looking after them, they all looked like rats with wings. But once I got to know them, they started to look different. Now even the weird ones look spectacular to me.

*ANIKA points out the pigeons by name.*

Jane Fonda, Kamala Harris, Julia … ? Yep, that's Julia Gillard. Marcia Langton, Joan of Arc, Germaine Greer, Rosa Parks, Marion Mahony Griffin—

ROSE: … Who?

ANIKA: Architect. Google her, and the one with the big tail feathers is Taylor Swift, and—watch out here comes Jacqui Lambie.

ROSE: Are there any boys?

ANIKA: Pigeons don't subscribe to gender norms, both sexes take on equal parenting duties, they both produce milk, and they mate for life. Together till the day they die.

*All of a sudden ROSE freezes.*

You okay?

ROSE: No. Pigeon on my head.

ANIKA: Relax, take it as a compliment, they don't land on your head unless they like you. That one doesn't have a name actually. What's your middle name?

ROSE: Olympia.

ANIKA: Perfect! Rose Olympia Livingstone Junior.

ROSE: Don't name it after me—

ANIKA: Why not?

ROSE: What if it flies off and never comes back?

ANIKA: It's a homing pigeon—

ROSE: Yeah but what if it gets injured?

ANIKA: I'll look after it.

ROSE: But what if—

ANIKA: What if Rose Olympia Livingstone turns out to be a champion and wins the sixty-mile sprint?

ROSE: What if she comes last?

ANIKA: The birds that come last are more incredible than the ones that win, Rose.

They go way off course, make all sorts of wrong choices yet they still manage to get home. Sometimes they are only one day behind the winning bird but they have flown twice the distance. Rose Olympia—

ROSE: Don't name it after me, okay!

*Beat.*

ANIKA: You know what the hardest thing about pigeon racing is, Rosie?

ROSE: Cleaning up their poo?

ANIKA: No, it's the waiting for them to come home.

ANIKA *picks up a feather.*

I saw you running after your dad's car last week.

ROSE: I was going for a jog.

ANIKA: In your PJs?

ROSE: It's a free country!

ROSE *starts to exit.*

ANIKA: Hey, take this.

ANIKA *offers* ROSE *a feather.*

As a reminder.

ROSE: For what?

ANIKA: To be kind to yourself.

*Pause.*

What? I'm not allowed to give you a feather in a free country?

ROSE *takes the feather.*

You don't have to choose me, but choose someone to talk to.

*Beat.*

So will I see you tomorrow?

ROSE: What time?

ANIKA: Our girl should be flying in round five.

ROSE *leaves and then doubles back. Pause.*

ROSE: You.

ANIKA: What?

ROSE: Can I choose you to talk to?

ANIKA: Okay—

ROSE: But you'll have to wait ... I ... I haven't got the words yet.

ANIKA: That's okay, I'm good at waiting.

*Beat.*

Thank you.

ROSE: What for?

ANIKA: Everyone likes to be chosen, Rose.

ANIKA *gives* ROSE *another feather.*

I want you to take really good care of this one because it is a future feather.

ROSE: What do you mean by that?

ANIKA: There will be a time, it's probably not going to be for a while ... if you are anything like me you will probably try all sorts of whack habits before you get to this time. But trust me, there will be a time when you look at this feather and you'll think—Anika was right.

ROSE: About what?

ANIKA: You're going to get through this, Rose. Trust me.

*SCENE FIVE—POWER CUT*

*Déjà Do Hair Salon.*

LIZ *is sitting in a chair with a cape on, looking into the mirror.* CINDY *stands behind her. (Note: Cindy looks remarkably like Pigeon.) Their conversation is conducted via the mirror reflection.*

CINDY: Outrageous!

LIZ: Well, if you look at the statistics it is actually pretty normal. Divorce rates are—

CINDY: So, what are you going to do?

LIZ: I don't know.

CINDY: Well let's start by giving you a take-no-shit haircut—

LIZ: I actually just want a trim, Cindy.

CINDY: We can do better than 'just a trim'.

LIZ: Mmmmm.

CINDY: People walk around thinking hair is just this stuff that grows on your head, but it's not. Get the right hairstyle, and you are literally carrying an ally on your head. Your hair is your ammo.

LIZ: I don't need ammo. As painful as it is, Marcus and I have finally laid down our guns.

CINDY: Then we need to go with a reinvention look. How about we do tapering découpage autumnal colour right through to the roots with a neo-brutal uneven bob cut coupled with low-fade highlights, razor-teeth bangs and a high-gloss keratin finish! Boom!

LIZ: … ?

CINDY: They call it the mic-drop cut.

> CINDY *drops the hairbrush she is holding, then quickly retrieves it.*

Just trust me, Liz.

LIZ: … I really did just want a trim.

CINDY: Sometimes, it is not about what you want, Liz, sometimes it is about what you need.

LIZ: I need to be able to pay the bills and get a bloody meal on the table every night, I need to feel like I am not letting my kids down. I need my marriage to not fall apart. And don't even start me on what I want. I want to look like I did ten years ago!

CINDY: I understand. Bad things happen to good people. And sometimes good things happen to bad people.

LIZ: Yep—

CINDY: And good people do bad things, and sometimes bad people do good things.

And sometimes good people get confused and think they are bad people, and sometimes bad people think they are good people and—

LIZ: I think I get the picture, thanks Cindy.

> CINDY *suddenly swivels* LIZ's *chair to face her.*

CINDY: I don't think you do get the picture, Liz. You are a beautiful person, you deserve good things.

> CINDY *swivels the chair back to the mirror.* LIZ *takes herself in.*

LIZ: I promised myself I'd tell the kids tomorrow.

CINDY: You can do it Liz.

LIZ: Not sure.

CINDY: Trust me, with this cut you can.

*CINDY shows LIZ a picture of a haircut from a magazine.*

LIZ: You really think I could pull that off?

CINDY: Yes, I do. Sit back, strap yourself in and get ready for your hair to do the work. You got this, and if you don't, your hair does.

*Blackout. CINDY puts on Pigeon's helmet and switches the flashlight on.*

## SCENE SIX—DREAM WORLD

*Rose's bedroom—night.*

ROSE *is sitting up in bed.* PIGEON *has her headlight pointing directly at* ROSE.

PIGEON: Your answer please?

ROSE: I don't know?

PIGEON: I'll give you a hint, heartbreak can be broken down into two elements.

ROSE: Can't we just drop the heartbreak question and go flying?

PIGEON: No. What is heartbreak? Your answer please?

ROSE: It's a very personal question.

PIGEON: Dreams are a personal medium.

*Beat.*

Okay, listen up because I am not going to repeat myself. Heartbreak is the moment when two things happen at once. One: you understand you need to let go, and two: you realise you can't let go. Got it?

ROSE: Heartbreak is the moment you understand you need to let go and realise you can't.

PIGEON: You got it, kid, see ya—

ROSE: Wait, what do I do with that information?

PIGEON: Simple. You concentrate on not letting it pull you apart, and when you feel strong enough, you help other people that are getting pulled apart. See ya.

*PIGEON takes off but misses the window.*

Goddamn it—I'm fine, I'm fine, just misfired … again!

*Attempt two. This time* PIGEON *makes it.*

YES!!!!! COME ON!

*SCENE SEVEN—SKY GAZING*

*Alan's backyard.*

*The sound of pigeons.* BEN, ANIKA, ALAN, XAVIER *and* ROSE *are looking skyward waiting for a homing pigeon to arrive.* XAVIER *is in and out, taking time out to look down at his phone.*

ANIKA *and* ALAN *have binoculars that go on and off their faces throughout the scene.*

BEN *and* XAVIER *are fearful of the pigeons. Their movements to avoid them escalate throughout the scene.*

BEN *thinks he has spotted the homing pigeon.*

BEN: There!
ALAN: Where?
BEN: There—
ALAN: WHERE, THERE?
BEN: THERE, THERE!
ALAN: THERE, WHERE?
BEN: THERE!
ALAN: NO! AND STOP YELLING!

> *Beat.*

You need your eyes checked! That's a currawong.
BEN: Is anybody else getting itchy? I think I'm allergic to them.
XAVIER: I am a bit itchy.
BEN: Alan, have these birds got mange?!??!
ALAN: No!

> BEN *sneezes, followed in quick succession by* XAVIER *burping.* BEN *ducks to protect his head from a swoop.*

XAVIER: How long do we have to wait?
ALAN: How long would it take you to travel two hundred miles on your own steam?
XAVIER: Don't know—
BEN: I do, it would take exactly one hundred and sixty minutes!

ALAN: In a car! These birds are powered by nothing but wings and heart! [*To* XAVIER] Put that away, you won't see her come in if you've got your nose in your phone. Have some respect, this bird will have battled phone towers, budget airlines, wind farms, inclement weather, lunatics that write religious messages in the sky and terrorists.

ROSE: Terrorists?

ALAN: Hawks, falcons, eagles.

BEN: Look at this Anika, I'm getting a rash from them.

ANIKA: Ohh, looks cute.

BEN: … What?

> *Another sighting.*

XAVIER: Is that it?

ALAN: No—

BEN: Yes—

XAVIER: There!

ALAN: Drone!

XAVIER: Cool!

ALAN: Magpie!

ROSE: Unicorn.

ALAN: What?

ROSE: That cloud looks like a unicorn!

ANIKA: Total unicorn, and that one looks like a fish. And that one looks like a seahorse—

ROSE: On a skateboard—

ANIKA: Totally. And that one—

ALAN: Enough! We are not looking at the clouds!

BEN: Well, technically we are looking at the clouds Alan—

ALAN: We are looking for a two-year-old Portuguese Tumbler hen homing pigeon!

Coming from the east! Or if she has really stuffed up from the south. I am not interested in hearing about bloody unicorns, currawongs, crows, drones, kites or any other rubbish! Have I made myself clear? Good! Thank you. Now, can everyone please shut up and focus on the task at hand!

> *Pause.*

BEN: This rash is moving toward my airways, Anika.

ANIKA: Breathe and relax—

> BEN *ducks then skips sideways.*

Breathe and visualise the pigeons as your friends.

> BEN *spots two pigeons mating.*

BEN: Oh my God, are those ones … ?
XAVIER: Disgusting!

> XAVIER *starts filming the pigeons.*

BEN: I can't unsee that.
XAVIER: Totally gross.
BEN: Get a room! Filthy—
XAVIER: So gross!
BEN: Absolutely, filthy.
ALAN: Shut up! And put that phone away Xavier!

> BEN *suddenly ducks and weaves in a panic.*

XAVIER: Great! One of them just shat on me! I'll probably get rabies now—
ALAN: Good! Payback for filming their private business. Now I've lost my binoculars! You've made me lose my—where are my bloody binoculars—Ben, did you take them?
BEN: No!
ANIKA: They're around—
ALAN: Someone has stolen them!
ROSE: They're around your neck.
ALAN: Thank you, Rose.

> *Beat.*

Nice to see someone has my back. [*To* BEN] I'm watching you.
BEN: That's it. I'm done.

> *Beat.*

Anika, you coming?
ALAN: Off you go, Anika.
ANIKA: You liberate a pigeon, you have to wait at the other end, that's the deal. It's bad karma not to wait—
BEN: I thought we were going to watch a movie together.
ANIKA: Yes, after our bird comes in.
BEN: But—

ANIKA *cuts* BEN *off with a long kiss, too long for a public kiss,* XAVIER *is mesmerised by it.*

ALAN: Eyes up Xavier!

*Pause.*

For the love of the sweet baby Jesus, shut it down, you two—go!

*Finally, the kiss ends.*

ANIKA: Later.

BEN *leaves, confused.*

ALAN: You're wasting your kissing talents hanging round here, go—

ANIKA: Is that her?

ALAN: No. That's your avoidance technique flying through the sky in fluorescent colours.

XAVIER: Where?

ALAN: Only visible to those who know her well, Xav.

BEN *doubles back.*

BEN: By the way, Alan—

ALAN: Here we go—

BEN: I would never steal your binoculars because I would never want to see the world the way you do. While you're sitting here looking into the distance, you're missing what is right in front of you. You think Anika would be spending every minute of her day looking after these birds if you weren't sick?

ANIKA: Ben!

ALAN: Well, would you?

ANIKA: Drop it!

BEN *leaves. Pause.*

ALAN: What's everybody looking at? The bird is coming in from the sky, so heads up and stop gawking.

ROSE: Sorry.

ANIKA *reaches down without looking away from her binoculars and takes* ROSE*'s hand.*

ALAN: Come on, little one, where are you?

ANIKA: You alright, Dad?

ALAN: No! She should be home by now. And before anyone opens their cakehole, that's an Eastern Spinebill.

*Beat.*

Common Myna. Crested pigeon, not my girl.

*Beat.*

Raven! Where the hell is she?

*Beat.*

I haven't got time for this.

ANIKA: You want to go in?

ALAN: No! I want this bird to get a bloody wriggle on, before I drop off the perch.

*Beat.*

And I want you to get a life.

ANIKA: Come on, Dad, I'll keep watch and clock her time when she comes in.

ALAN: This may be the last one I see come home. Come on, little one, come home.

*Everyone looks up.*

BEN *re-enters.*

BEN: Look, Alan, I am sorry, but—

ALAN: Shut up and look up.

BEN *follows instructions.*

ROSE *steps forward and addresses the audience.*

ROSE: We were in a staring match with the sky. And I wished I could hide away in that waiting game forever.

*Pause.*

But the longer we waited the more I felt it pulling at me, and it takes over everything—sleeping, eating, even breathing. Even the cracks in the pavement. I count how many I step on, like it could change things. Like I could make a deal that lets me count the world back into shape.

*Beat.*

If that pigeon flies through a cloud before I count to ten, everything will be alright, Alan will get better, Ben and Anika will stay together, Mum won't go crazy with her hair, Xavier will win the stupid Birdman Rally, and my dad will come back.

*Pause.*

One, two, three, four, five, six, seven, eight, nine ... nine, ten.

*Beat.*

Eleven, twelve, thirteen—So, I start again. One, two, three—and with every number, I can feel it coming to get me, four, five—and it has me, the pulled apart feeling, the need to let go and hold on at the same time.

LIZ *calls from off stage.*

LIZ: Rosie, Xav.

XAVIER *takes off.*

ROSE: It is here, Xav knows it and so do I. Six, seven, eight—

LIZ: Xavier, Rose!

ROSE: It's in her voice.

LIZ: Rose!

ROSE: Nine, ten, eleven—

ALAN: Rose! Your mum!

ROSE: Twelve, thirteen—

ANIKA: Got your feathers?

ROSE: Yep.

ANIKA *lets go of* ROSE *'s hand.*

ALAN: Off you go now, Rosie.

ROSE *musters her courage and exits.*

Jesus!

BEN: What?

ALAN: That rash has taken a turn for the worse.

BEN: Really?

ANIKA: Dad—

ALAN: Go have a look in the mirror, your face is bright purple!

BEN: Really?

ALAN: I think you're on the way out, son.

BEN: Jesus!

BEN *exits.*

ALAN: I'm leaving my birds to him when I go.

ANIKA: Very funny—

ALAN: And my lifetime subscription to *Pigeon Fancier.* He does have a point, you wouldn't be wasting your time looking after the birds if I wasn't like this.

ANIKA: Is that her?

ALAN: Don't change the subject. Looking after these birds isn't going to change things.

ANIKA: Not as though you can look after them.

> *Beat.*

ALAN: You were more fun when you went out till all hours and I was the one that had to tell you what day it was. Go and watch a movie with whatshisname.

ANIKA: Ben.

ALAN: Ben the hypochondriac.

ANIKA: Is that her?

ALAN: No.

> *Beat.*

If the bird doesn't come in it is not your fault, they belong to nature, once you let them go there is nothing you can do.

> *Beat.*

Even if she does come in, she's lost the race.

ANIKA: It's only six o'clock.

ALAN: She won't even place—

ANIKA: Stop being a pessimist—

ALAN: I'm a realist.

> *Beat.*

The doctor told me I've got six weeks.

ANIKA: …

ALAN: Don't go the way I did when your mum died. Doesn't work. Let yourself be loved … even if it is by the hypochondriac. Now is the time, Anika, before I get worse.

> *Beat.*

Off you go, I'll be fine.

ANIKA: Call me if you need me—

ALAN: I'll call you when our bird comes in.

ANIKA: Dad—

ALAN: Go!

*SCENE EIGHT—THE TRUTH*

*Liz's house.*

LIZ *is sporting an abrasive new haircut, it's a real fright, and* ROSE *cannot stop staring at it.*

LIZ: It will grow out.

> LIZ *pulls a feather from* ROSE*'s hair.* ROSE *takes the feather off her mother.*

I understand horse racing, dog racing, even crab racing, but pigeon racing?

ROSE: What's wrong with it?

LIZ: I am not saying there is anything wrong with it, Rose, I just find it odd for an eighteen-year-old woman to be involved in pigeon racing. I thought all pigeon people were lonely boozy old men.

ROSE: Anika said she's a trailblazer.

LIZ: In the pigeon world?

ROSE: Yep.

> ROSE *starts drawing on the table with the feather. Her mother observes the line of her hand.*

LIZ: What are you drawing?

ROSE: Nothing.

> *Beat.*

LIZ: Remember how we used to draw on each other's back and try and guess—tree!

ROSE: No.

LIZ: Yes, that's the trunk and that's the branches—

ROSE: It's not a tree!

LIZ: Dog! You're drawing a dog!

ROSE: No!

*LIZ gets up, walks to the end of the room and calls out to her son.*

LIZ: Xavier!

ROSE: He'll be in the shed.

*LIZ walks across to the other side of the room, she opens the glass sliding doors and calls out to the backyard.*

LIZ: Xavier! He has five more minutes and I'm going in.

ROSE: You have to knock.

LIZ: What?

ROSE: Dad was the only one allowed in. He thinks it's bad luck if people see his stupid flying machine.

LIZ: Did you tell him it was important?

ROSE: Yes, I said: 'It's important. Mum wants to have a "family talk", and she's been to Déjà Do, that's how important it is.'

*LIZ calls loudly.*

LIZ: Xavier!

*Beat.*

XAVIER! What is wrong with that boy?

ROSE: Lots—

LIZ: Don't start. XAVIER! XAVIER!

*A despondent XAVIER appears through the glass doors and sits at the table. He is glued to his phone.*

Xavier, when your sister tells you I want to talk to you—put down your phone please.

XAVIER: One minute—

LIZ: Now—

XAVIER: Just give me a minute.

*LIZ takes the phone off XAVIER.*

Mum!

*XAVIER spots ROSE's feather.*

Those birds are filthy—

ROSE: You're filthy—

LIZ: Okay—

*ROSE touches her brother's face with the feather.*

XAVIER: Err, disgusting—

LIZ: Rose!

XAVIER: She's trying to give me rabies—

ROSE: You've already got rabies!

XAVIER: Yeah from you, you invented rabies.

ROSE: You are rabies.

> ROSE *again tries to touch* XAVIER *with the feather.*

LIZ: Enough—

XAVIER: How come you take my phone but you don't take her feather?

LIZ: Give me the feather, Rose—

> ROSE *again tries to touch* XAVIER *with the feather.*

LIZ: STOP IT!

XAVIER: SHE STARTED IT!

ROSE: DID NOT!

LIZ: YOUR FATHER AND I ARE SEPARATING!

> *Everything stops as the words sink in.*

ROSE: One, two, three, four—

LIZ: Rosie …

XAVIER: Weirdo.

LIZ: Xavier!

XAVIER: She's doing that counting thing again—

LIZ: And you are locking yourself in that bloody shed building a flying machine.

> You're just as weird.

> *Beat.*

Sorry. Your father and I—

> ROSE *takes the feather from the centre of the table.*

XAVIER: You're always separating.

LIZ: No, Xav, we are always falling apart and patching over it. This is different.

> *Pause.*

You can't split happiness or sadness into neat little compartments, we tried to do that for a long time, and it didn't work or we failed, I don't know which. We probably failed.

*Beat.*

So … if you have any questions?

*Beat.*

Anything, anytime. You just go ahead.

*Beat.*

When you're ready. Alright.

*Beat.*

So, I thought we might have pizza tonight.

ROSE: Where is he going to live?

LIZ: I don't know … Would you rather fish and chips?

ROSE: Where is he?

LIZ: I told you, Rose, I don't know.

XAVIER *gets up.*

Xavier—sit down!

XAVIER: Why?

LIZ: Because I need you, so sit!

XAVIER *sits. Pause.*

XAVIER: Is he going to live with Joanne?

LIZ: Xavier!

ROSE: Who is Joanne?

XAVIER: Is he?

LIZ: …

ROSE: Who is Joanne?

ROSE *picks the feather up again.*

LIZ: Rosie. I was going to tell you, but you—can you please put that feather down!

LIZ *takes the feather off* ROSE.

*BANG! Something hits the window. Everyone freezes.*

Stay calm.

LIZ *approaches the window. Beat.* ANIKA *appears and startles* LIZ.

Oh my God!

ANIKA, *barges in holding Pigeon Rose Olympia Livingstone.*

ANIKA: Have you got a towel?

LIZ: What?

ANIKA: Tea towel, anything, I just need something to wrap—

ROSE *grabs her mother's coat off the back of her chair.*

Perfect.

LIZ: That's my work jacket.

ANIKA: Thanks, Mrs Livingstone.

ANIKA *gently wraps the pigeon up in the coat and sits at the kitchen table next to* ROSE.

Poor pigeon, obviously got disorientated. Easy mistake, I've done it, who hasn't run into a glass door? But this is my fault, I pushed her too hard.

*She rests the pigeon on her lap.*

ROSE: Is it dead?

ANIKA: No. You're going to be okay, you just need to get over the shock, Rose Olympia Livingstone.

ROSE: I told you not to name it after me—

XAVIER: No wonder it crashed.

LIZ: Xavier!

*Beat.*

Anika—

ANIKA: Nice haircut, Mrs Livingstone.

LIZ: It just needs to settle in.

ANIKA: No, the unsettled look suits you. So how is everyone?

LIZ: Good—

XAVIER: Crap—

LIZ: Xavier! How are you Anika?

ANIKA: Good. Besides this incident. Really excellent.

*Beat.*

Black thanks, Mrs Livingstone.

LIZ: Sorry?

ANIKA: Black with no sugar.

LIZ: … Anika, I didn't offer you a cup of tea—

ANIKA: I thought you offered—I must be in shock. Dad would kill me if he knew about this. He is always telling me not to push the birds before they're ready. Ironic, because he is so bossy. I'd just love him to see one of his birds win the two hundred sprint before—you know ... before summer ends.

*Beat.*

LIZ: How is your dad?

ANIKA: Good. Forget the coffee, Mrs Livingstone, I could go straight to a glass of wine.

LIZ: Look, Anika, I'm—I'm very sorry your pigeon has had an accident but we were kind of in the middle of something here.

ANIKA: Right, sorry. Just pretend I am not here and as soon as she comes good, I'll skip out. As you were.

LIZ: Anika—we were in the middle of a sensitive family discussion. So ... I am going to have to ask you to—

XAVIER: Mum and Dad are separating—

LIZ: Xavier!?!?

XAVIER: Dad is going to live with his new girlfriend.

ROSE: What?

XAVIER *exits. Pause.*

ANIKA: Oh wow, I mean not wow but okay. Not okay but—

LIZ: Anika!

ANIKA: Sorry to have interrupted, Mrs Livingstone. I'll go now.

ANIKA *gets up to leave.*

Unless—are you sure you wouldn't like that glass of wine? Have you got wine? I could go get some—

LIZ: No.

ANIKA: Okay. Anytime though. Thanks, Mrs Livingstone.

LIZ: My coat.

ANIKA: What?

LIZ: Your pigeon is wrapped in my coat—

ANIKA: Right, I will bring it back.

LIZ: And would you mind—can you get it dry cleaned, please. If that's okay?

ANIKA: Totally.

LIZ: Okay.

ANIKA: Okay, and I'm sorry. And your hair looks great.

LIZ: Thank you.

ANIKA: Okay. Bye then.

LIZ: Yep. Bye.

> ANIKA *starts to leave and doubles back.*

ANIKA: Sorry, Mrs Livingstone, just one more thing. Remember what I told you Rosie, okay?

ROSE: … What?

ANIKA: If my pigeon gets injured I'm going to look after it. [*To the pigeon*] You're going to be fine, Rose Olympia Livingstone.

ROSE: Easy for you to say.

LIZ: I think Anika was talking to the pigeon, Rose.

> ANIKA *moves her head close to Pigeon Rose Olympia Livingstone.*

ANIKA: What?

> ANIKA *pretends to listen to Pigeon Rose Olympia.*

She said she's going to smash the sixty-mile sprint once she grows up.

ROSE: Did not.

ANIKA: No, but she's going to be okay.

ROSE: How do you know?

> *Beat.*

ANIKA: [*to* ROSE] Feel her heartbeat?

LIZ: Go on.

> ANIKA *indicates where to place her finger.*

ANIKA: Just here.

> ROSE *places her fingers on her namesake's heart.*

ANIKA: Feel that?

ROSE: Yep.

ANIKA: Count it for me, so I know she's okay.

> *Pause.* ANIKA *looks at* LIZ *and they both get on board.*

You counting?

ROSE: Yep.

LIZ: Out loud, Rose, so Anika knows she's okay.

ROSE: Eleven, twelve, thirteen, fourteen, fifteen.

LIZ: Does that sound okay?

ANIKA: Yep. She'll be fine.

*Beat.*

Thanks, and sorry for interrupting, Mrs Livingstone—

LIZ: Liz.

ANIKA: Liz.

ANIKA *leaves. Pause.*

LIZ: You can't say she's not an unusual girl, Rose.

ROSE: Yeah, I know but she can drive those birds miles away from their home to a place they don't know, and even if it takes them days or weeks to find their way, they come home. Even though all sorts of things can happen to them on the way, helicopters, mobile phone towers, wind farms, lunatics that write things in the sky, and terrorists.

LIZ: Terrorists?

ROSE: Yeah, like hawks or eagles.

*Beat.*

Joanne?

LIZ: She's not a terrorist, Rose. Your father has many faults, but I don't think he would fall for a terrorist.

*Pause.*

I'm sorry I didn't tell you your dad had a girlfriend.

ROSE: Anika told me sometimes a pigeon can stuff up and go the wrong way and make all sorts of mistakes but they still come home.

LIZ: Your dad will come back, Rose, but he is not going to live here anymore.

ROSE: Anika also told me that pigeons have the same partner for life, like forever.

And ever. They're monotonous.

LIZ: Monogamous.

*Pause.*

So fish and chips or pizza?

ROSE: Turn sideways.

LIZ *follows instructions.* ROSE *draws on* LIZ *'s back with the feather.*

LIZ: Bird?

ROSE: No.

LIZ: Hills?

ROSE: No.

LIZ: Hint?

ROSE: It should be easy. I'll start again, concentrate.

LIZ: Love heart!

ROSE: Way off—

LIZ: Well draw better—

ROSE: And you wonder why I don't do this stupid stuff anymore—

LIZ: Shhhh, I'm concentrating … Moon and stars?

ROSE: No. Close.

> *Beat.*

Pizza.

LIZ: You want pizza?

ROSE: I haven't finished yet. Pizza and fish and chips.

LIZ: You want both? That's a lot.

ROSE: You might need it.

LIZ: Why would I need—

ROSE: Emotional eating.

LIZ: What about pizza, garlic bread and a hug?

> LIZ *puts her arms out. Pause.*

You want those chips?

ROSE: I want things to be like they used to be.

LIZ: I know, that's why I want to give you a hug. You're going to have to stop chasing your dad's car every time he comes and goes. You'll end up outrunning him, his cars are always such shitboxes.

> *Beat.*

Come here.

> LIZ *puts her arms out.*

No hug, no pizza.

> ROSE *reluctantly hugs her mother. Once in the embrace she surrenders to it.*

When you were little the border to Rosieville was always open.

LIZ *lets* ROSE *out of her embrace.*

You're a good hugger, Rose Olympia, you should let your guard down more often.

ROSE: You should have ignored Cindy, you don't need to ... what does she call it?

LIZ: Reinvent myself ... It's terrible isn't it.

ROSE: ... Yeah.

LIZ: You could lie.

ROSE: Okay, it's really pretty, frames your face perfectly, and really suits you.

LIZ: Cindy's ... she is a lovely girl but ... well ...

ROSE: She can't cut hair for shit.

LIZ: Rose!

*SCENE NINE—RELAX*

*Ben's house.*

BEN *is sitting on a chair, blindfolded.*

BEN: I thought we were going to watch a movie together tonight?

ANIKA: Relax—

    ANIKA *places a box on* BEN's *lap.*

BEN: What the hell is this? Shit something's—there is something moving—what is this?

    *A muffed coo comes from inside the box.*

Holy shit!

ANIKA: Breathe—

BEN: What are you doing?

ANIKA: Try and relax, or the pigeon—

BEN: I knew it! I am allergic to pigeons—

ANIKA: Only in your mind—

BEN: What?

ANIKA: I am going to cure you of your allergies.

BEN: No, you're going to inflame them.

ANIKA: It's called pigeon aversion therapy. If it works I am going to make an app, sell it all over the world. It will go off in Venice.

BEN: How many wines have you had?

ANIKA: Two—four—I don't know. Shut up—Just be open and listen, listen to this audio presentation by Anika—

BEN: You're not an audio presentation, Anika—

ANIKA: Yes, I am, I just forgot the music.

BEN: Anika!

ANIKA: Shhhhh!

> ANIKA *puts on some Philip Glass-type music.*

BEN: Oh God here we go.

ANIKA: Welcome to my hypnosis audio presentation, soon to be best-selling pigeon aversion app. Yeah baby! Sorry ... relax. By the end of this meditation—hypnosis—all your pigeon fear will be gone—sound good?

BEN: No!

ANIKA: Let us begin. Take yourself to the place where you feel confronted by a pigeon—

BEN: Like right here, right now.

ANIKA: Imagine—

BEN: Don't have to imagine, I have a pigeon on my lap!

ANIKA: See the moment when you feel you are at risk of being assaulted by a pigeon—

BEN: Okay, now I am itchy—

ANIKA: Take three deep breaths—

BEN: This is how it starts—so itchy—

ANIKA: Allow your lungs to fill with all your redundant fear and release it all, and breathe in, assured in the knowledge that pigeons are friendly animals, so what's the problem—

BEN: Itchy, that's the problem, that and you. You're the problem, Anika—

ANIKA: Just breathe. One, two, three and rest. And now ask yourself, are my fears based in fact or are they just super stupid ideas? And ask yourself, am I a hypochondriac who is constantly blaming pigeons—

BEN: Okay, that is enough—Can we stop?

ANIKA: We can stop when you stop blaming pigeons for your itchy problems and you take responsibility.

BEN: You're the one that needs to take responsibility.

ANIKA: Shhhh, we are not talking about me. We are talking about pigeons!

BEN: I don't want to talk about pigeons, I'm sick of pigeons!

ANIKA: Because you don't understand them. They are smart, magnificent— they can understand numbers, remember faces and they were used in wars to send messages and spot survivors on sinking ships. Amazing! They rescue people! Pigeons are heroes, rescue heroes—

BEN: You need rescuing—

> BEN *takes his blindfold off.*

Get it off me.

> *Beat.*

And turn off the tinkle-tinkle music.

> ANIKA *removes the pigeon from* BEN*'s lap.*

ANIKA: You'll regret this when my app takes off!

BEN: Anika, this is going to hurt so I am going to 'breathe in my fear' and say it as honestly as I can. You are crap at looking after pigeons, the one from last night is still not back, this one keeps running into glass doors. And several of them have turned on each other since you started looking after them—

ANIKA: It takes time.

BEN: You haven't got time, Anika. So you are going to have to find another way to tell your dad you love him before he dies. And stop trying to fix me, I am allergic to pigeons, can't help it. And I am in love with you, can't help that either.

> *Pause.*

ANIKA: I don't know.

BEN: Put the pigeon in its coop.

ANIKA: Then what?

BEN: Then come back, and I'll find the saddest movie available, and you can curl up on my couch and bawl your eyes out, no questions asked. How about we start there?

ANIKA: It will have to be really sad …

BEN: Anika, you cried at a tissue ad the other day, I think I know where the bar sits.

## SCENE TEN—THE BUILD

*The shed.*

BEN *walks in wearing a T-shirt with 'Team Déjà Do' written on it.*

BEN: Good news, Déjà Do is sponsoring us!

XAVIER: What? No-one asked me. What does that mean?

BEN: Free T-shirt. Put it on.

> BEN *throws* XAVIER *a T-shirt.*

And free haircuts for your family for a year.

XAVIER: Have you seen my mum's hair?

BEN: Is it as bad as everyone says?

XAVIER: Yes, it scares small animals. Where's Alan?

BEN: Sponsorship makes us look good even if it means nothing.

XAVIER: What does Alan think about it?

BEN: He is all for it.

XAVIER: Yeah but look at his hair.

BEN: Where are we up to here?

XAVIER: I don't know, that's why we need Alan. Where is he?

BEN: You just got me today, Xav, so what needs to be done?

XAVIER: I don't know, let's wait for Alan.

BEN: He wants us to keep working, you know what he is like.

> *Beat.*

So what's next?

XAVIER: Will he come tomorrow?

BEN: I don't know. So, let's just get on with it—

XAVIER: Is Alan alright?

> *Pause.*

BEN: He was admitted to hospital last night.

> *Beat.*

If we keep working it's going to make it easier.

> *Beat.*

So what's next?

XAVIER: I was kind of relying on Alan to tell me how to do the next bit.
BEN: And now he is relying on you, so it is time to step up, Xavier.

> *Beat.*

The best thing you can do at the moment is finish this. Make Alan feel as though he helped you achieve something.
XAVIER: He kind of bullied me into it.
BEN: What do you think I'm doing here? So, what were we up to?
XAVIER: The part that holds you in place.
BEN: The harness, yes?
XAVIER: Yep.

> *Beat.*

Do you think Alan is afraid of dying?
BEN: Bloody hell, Xavier.
XAVIER: I would be afraid. I'm a ... I'm a bit afraid of flying.
BEN: How about we put some bars out the front of the harness, like a sort of steering wheel, so you can hold on and feel like you have some control?
XAVIER: I am going to need something to hold on to.

*SCENE ELEVEN—DREAM WORLD*

*Rosieville.*

PIGEON: Thank you for coming my way. So what do you think of Rosieville? It's nothing flash but it's home to me.
ROSE: Needs a bit of a clean-up.
PIGEON: Well, you abandon a place for too long and this is what happens.
ROSE: Can I ask you a question this time?
PIGEON: Knock yourself out.
ROSE: Do you have rabies?
PIGEON: No.
ROSE: Mange?
PIGEON: That I do have, I'm riddled with it. It's a good thing, proves I've lived.
Speaking of living, I think you're ready.
ROSE: For what ... ?

PIGEON: Would you like to fly?

ROSE: Can I … I was wondering if you could give me a flying credit.

PIGEON: You don't feel ready yet?

ROSE: No, I need it for my brother, he is entering the Birdman and—

PIGEON: Say no more. It is done. I love the Birdman, trying to watch people do what we do. All us birds love it, we think it is hilarious. Humans fly like bricks.

> PIGEON *starts writing out a flying credit.*

ROSE: That's why I need the credit.

PIGEON: Okay. One transferable flight credit. How far?

ROSE: Anything over fifty metres will do.

PIGEON: Going for the big bucks hey? Fifty-five-point-two metres.

> PIGEON *hands the credit to* ROSE.

ROSE: Thank you. Do you … Will you … ?

PIGEON: Spit it out?

ROSE: Will this work? Do you work outside of my head?

PIGEON: That is what life is, waiting to see if things work outside of your head.

ROSE: But will it work?

PIGEON: I don't know, ask Carl Jung!

ROSE: Who's he?

PIGEON: He's my second cousin twice removed, he taught me everything I know, really smart guy.

> ROSE *itches.*

ROSE: I think I might be getting your mange.

> PIGEON *suddenly claps, startling* ROSE.

PIGEON: Bastard!

ROSE: What?

PIGEON: That's what's making you itch. Mosquito!

ROSE: Really.

PIGEON: Yep, Rosieville is a bloody jungle.

ROSE: What is a pigeon doing in a jungle? Pigeons aren't tropical?

PIGEON: Yeah and humans aren't meant to fly, so shut your mouth. This is a jungle!

ROSE: … okay!

PIGEON: It's a metaphor, Rose.
ROSE: A what?
PIGEON: You'll figure it out. See ya.

## SCENE TWELVE—THE RETURN

*Anika's bedroom.*

ANIKA *is in bed with the covers over her head.*

ROSE: Trust me.
ANIKA: No.
ROSE: I know you will love it.
ANIKA: Rose, I'm really not up for going out yet.
ROSE: It's just the backyard.
ANIKA: Not ready.
ROSE: It's been three days—
ANIKA: Time doesn't work in days anymore. Just tell me, Rose.
ROSE: You won't believe it, unless you see it for yourself.
ANIKA: What?
ROSE: I didn't think it was possible, but Alan told me about that a pigeon during the war that had a leg—
ANIKA: Leg hanging off and a bullet in its breast—
ROSE: Yeah that one, it kept going, all broken and shot up, but it kept going until it crossed enemy lines.
ANIKA: That was its job, that's what it was trained to do.
ROSE: It saved a whole battalion.
ANIKA: I'm anti-war, Rose.
ROSE: So am I.
ANIKA: So don't start a fight with me.
ROSE: Remember how you told me the ones that come last are the most amazing. Don't you want to see it?
ANIKA: If you are just doing this to get me out of bed, I'll kill you, Rose.

    *Beat.*

ROSE: Just walk to the window. If it's not Alan's pigeon, I'll give you my future feather back.

    ANIKA *gets up and puts her sunglasses on.* ROSE *opens the curtains and stands at the window. Pause.*

ANIKA: Nice try, Rose.

ANIKA *makes her way back to bed.*

ROSE: Wait, Look, there!

ANIKA *turns back.*

ANIKA: Okay, I see it.

ROSE: It came back, after so long. Don't you think that is amazing—

ANIKA: Homing pigeons are amazing. No-one really knows how they do it.

*SCENE THIRTEEN—FLIGHT*

*Lake Burley Griffin.*

*Everyone in the ensemble is facing upstage looking skyward, except for* ANIKA. XAVIER *stands on a platform above wearing his Birdman machine. Everyone is wearing 'Team Déjà Do' T-shirts.*

COMMENTATOR: [*voiceover*] Why do things come back? That will be a big question on many people's lips today as we see the return of the Birdman Rally. Not since 1992 have we witnessed humans attempting to fly across Lake Burley Griffin. And for good reason, it is a ridiculous proposition yet here we are again, repeating what some would say is a bizarre chapter in our local history. And why are we doing this? I do not know. The human spirit is a mystery. I am just doing my job, commentating on my community. People say pigs can't fly, and today I think we will see humans also can't fly. Happy to be proved wrong but as things stand I believe we are again going to be faced with an idiotic event full of failure, falling and schadenfreude. So strap yourself in while we get on with it.

CINDY: Do you think Xavier can do it?

ROSE: Yep.

LIZ: Oh really? I thought you said his flying machine was stupid and he had rabies.

ROSE: You can still fly with rabies.

CINDY: What? My logo is all over this.

COMMENTATOR: [*voiceover*] Today's Birdman entrants are judged on costume, the personality of the dismount and the skill of the flyer. The ultimate winner is judged on distance.

ANIKA: Got your feather?
COMMENTATOR: [*voiceover*] All flyers face a common enemy—gravity.
ROSE: Yep.
COMMENTATOR: [*voiceover*] Ultimately every pilot's destination is the
    same, the water. And Mr Stewart Robinson from Reid is stepping
    up to the plate, and we have dismount ... but no, zero elevation.
    Once again, gravity is the winner.
CINDY: Oh God after seeing that, I am not so sure this is the right thing
    to attach my brand to.
ROSE: Xav is going to do it. Trust me.
COMMENTATOR: [*voiceover*] Next up is a Mr Xavier Livingstone from
    Belconnen, he is waiting while Mr Robinson is assisted out of the
    water.
BEN: Xavier's got this.
CINDY: What makes you so sure?
ROSE: This expert called Carl Jung, really smart guy, reckons he can
    do it.
COMMENTATOR: [*voiceover*] Mr Livingstone is warming up and taking
    this very seriously indeed. Great to see some new blood in the
    competition. He is sponsored by Déjà Do Hair Salon, and I can tell
    you Déjà Do is the place to go if you want something different.

    XAVIER *steps forward.*

    Mr Livingstone's vessel design is based on the Portuguese tumbler
    Pigeon, unusual choice, but it takes all sorts.
BEN: Go Xav!
CINDY: Team Déjà Do! Déjà Do! Déjà Do! Déjà Do!
LIZ: Okay, Cindy.
COMMENTATOR: [*voiceover*] And finally Mr Robinson has been cleared
    from the water. Mr Livingstone is stepping up to the plate.
CINDY: Déjà Do! DÉJÀ DO!
LIZ: CINDY!

    XAVIER *raises his wings.*

COMMENTATOR: [*voiceover*] And we have dismount. Great elevation,
    that's two metres, good speed, three metres. Four metres—well
    I never! We have a flyer!
CINDY: YES!

COMMENTATOR: [*voiceover*] Six metres! Using every bit of that twelve knots of wind—eight metres, and no sign of descent—Nine metres! ten metres!

ALAN: Go, tiger! Go!

ROSE: Eleven, twelve, thirteen, fourteen—

COMMENTATOR: [*voiceover*] On a wing and a prayer, look at him go!

ROSE *takes* ANIKA*'s hand.*

ALAN: Look up, Anika.

ROSE: It's all up there, you just have to remember to look up. There's sun, moon, clouds. Go, Xav!

ROSE *turns to address the audience.*

COMMENTATOR: [*voiceover*] This is why we do it!

ROSE: Unicorns, shooting stars, rainbows and a brother who, against all the odds, can fly—twenty-one, twenty-two, twenty-three—

CINDY: Fifty metres!

COMMENTATOR: [*voiceover*] Twenty-four, twenty-five, this is flight! This is what it is all about.

ROSE: Then there's lightning and storms for all the things you cannot control. Thirty-one, thirty-two. We are still waiting for Dad to come back.

COMMENTATOR: [*voiceover*] And he's nearly there! Forty-three—Is it a man? Is it a bird? No, this is Xavier Livingstone from Belco! The Birdman is back!

ROSE: Whole planets and universes that haven't even been discovered.

BEN *takes* ANIKA*'s other hand.*

ALAN: Look up.

LIZ: Come on, Xavier, you can do it!

ALL: Forty-four, forty-five, forty-six, forty-seven, forty-eight, forty-nine—FIFTY!

CINDY: Thank you, God!

COMMENTATOR: [*voiceover*] A man is flying! We have a flying man! Look at him go!

LIZ: That's my boy!

COMMENTATOR: [*voiceover*] And he's done it! He has broken the fifty-metre mark! Fifty-one! Fifty-two, Fifty-three—

CINDY: Alright that's enough—

COMMENTATOR: [*voiceover*] Fifty-four!

CINDY: SHUT IT DOWN!

LIZ: Cindy?!?!

CINDY: He got his fifty, shut it down. I am the chief sponsor, and I am saying enough now! Shut it down or I'm leaving!

COMMENTATOR: [*voiceover*] Fifty-five!

CINDY: That's it, I'm out!

> CINDY *exits.*

COMMENTATOR: [*voiceover*] Well that is a record, fifty-five-point-five! He has done it! Every single Canberran should be bursting at the seams with pride! Beat that, Moomba Birdman!

> XAVIER *lands, he takes his wings off and places them on* ALAN.

> ALAN *plucks a feather from the wings and hands it to* ANIKA.

> *He starts to make his way up to the birdman platform.*

> PIGEON *enters.*

PIGEON: Well your brother is definitely no brick!

ROSE: Thank you

PIGEON: What for?

ROSE: The flying credit?

PIGEON: Your idea. Congratulations!

ROSE: What for?

PIGEON: Things working out … outside your head.

> PIGEON *takes their helmet with flashlight off, and places it on* ROSE*'s head.*

ROSE: Why are you giving me this?

PIGEON: Because my work here is done. So, see ya.

ROSE: No.

> ROSE *takes the helmet off.*

PIGEON: You're no longer a mega job. I gotta move on to other jobs.

> *Beat.*

Rose, there are lots of other people out there that can't make the stuff in their head work.

> *Beat.*

So put the helmet on, and let's do this. Come on, trust yourself, Rose.

ROSE *puts the helmet on.*

On the count of three okay? Ready?

ROSE: No.

PIGEON: One, two, three—

*Beat.*

Come on, Rose, we can do this, I'll say it with you. One, two, three.

ROSE *and* PIGEON: Goodbye.

ROSE: Love you.

PIGEON: What?

ROSE: Nothing.

PIGEON: No, I think you might have said—

ROSE: As if, you've got mange!

PIGEON: Okay. See ya, rude girl.

PIGEON *clicks their fingers and lights snap to black as the headlight on* ROSE's *helmet switches on.*

ROSE: Alan died on Thursday last week, two days before his sixty-fifth birthday. The sky doesn't ask if you are ready for what is coming. Doesn't ask if you have all you need to get through another day. Sunset and sunrise just keep turning up. It just keeps happening, day upon day, and night upon night, constantly turning over and making this heartbreaking, strange, wonderful, terrible, boring, surprising, scary, horrendous, disappointing, joyous, amazing thing called your one and only life.

ALAN: Welcome to the jungle.

ALAN *raises his wings.*

# THE END

CANBERRA YOUTH THEATRE PRESENTS

# ROSIEVILLE

## BY MARY RACHEL BROWN

WORLD PREMIERE
**29 SEPTEMBER – 8 OCTOBER 2023**
THE COURTYARD STUDIO – CANBERRA THEATRE CENTRE

## CAST

| | |
|---|---|
| **ROSE** | IMOGEN BIGSBY-CHAMBERLIN |
| **XAVIER** | OSCAR ABRAHAM |
| **LIZ** | AMY CRAWFORD |
| **ALAN** | RICHARD MANNING |
| **ANIKA** | DISA SWIFTE |
| **BEN** | CALLUM DOHERTY |
| **PIGEON / CINDY** | CLAIRE IMLACH |

## CREATIVE TEAM

| | |
|---|---|
| **DIRECTOR** | LUKE ROGERS |
| **SET & COSTUME DESIGNER** | AISLINN KING |
| **LIGHTING DESIGNER** | ETHAN HAMILL |
| **SOUND DESIGNER & COMPOSER** | PATRICK HAESLER |
| **ASSISTANT DIRECTOR** | EMILY AUSTIN |
| **STAGE MANAGER** | RHILEY WINNETT |
| **ASSISTANT STAGE MANAGER** | HANNAH McGINNESS |

## ACKNOWLEDGEMENTS

We greatly acknowledge the support of the ACT Government through artsACT, and Ainslie and Gorman Arts Centres. This production is supported by Canberra Theatre Centre, as part of a commitment to nurturing the young and emerging artists of the ACT.

*Rosieville* was commissioned and developed by Canberra Youth Theatre.

# CANBERRA YOUTH THEATRE

## THE VOICE OF YOUTH EXPRESSED THROUGH CHALLENGING AND INTELLIGENT THEATRE

Canberra Youth Theatre is one of the leading youth arts companies in Australia.

We provide opportunities for young people to collaborate, develop their artistic skills and create pathways to the professional arts sector.

We advocate for and amplify the voices of young people, providing a space for them to discover and express their creative selves.

We produce powerful theatre where young artists ignite urgent conversations, challenge the forces that shape them, and invite us to see the world from new perspectives.

Over our 50 year history, we have collaborated with thousands of young artists through productions, workshops, creative developments and community events. We have created works in our major theatres, public spaces, and national cultural institutions. We have toured around the country, and internationally.

Canberra Youth Theatre has grown and evolved significantly over the past five decades, constantly responding to the passions and perspectives of generations of young people, and adapting to changes in the way we create and experience live performance. We remain at the forefront of Australian youth theatre practice, creating innovative, accessible and challenging opportunities for young people to access and engage in professional-quality theatrical experiences.

From Debra Oswald's now Australian classic *Dags*, and works by writers Tommy Murphy, Mary Rachel Brown, Lachlan Philpott, Angela Betzien, Liv Hewson, Ross Mueller, Emily Sheehan, Jessica Bellamy, Cathy Petocz, Julian Larnach, and Tasnim Hossain, we have nurtured new voices and commissioned professional artists to create acclaimed works for young people.

We continue to nurture and develop young people, giving them a place to belong, to share their voice, and to inspire audiences of all ages.

*Canberra Youth Theatre acknowledges the Ngunnawal and Ngambri peoples as the Traditional Owners of the lands on which we collaborate, share stories, and create art. We celebrate their rich history of over 60,000 years of culture and storytelling. We recognise their continuing connection to the lands and waters of our region. We pay our respects to their Elders past, present and emerging. Sovereignty was never ceded. Always was and always will be.*

*"You have to accept the fact that sometimes you are the pigeon, and sometimes you are the statue."* - Claude Chabrol

*Rosieville* examines the nature of waiting and how we hold ourselves together while looking down the barrel of uncertainty. I hope to capture some of the human anxieties, habits, and distractions we create to compensate for things not being how we want them to be. Ultimately *Rosieville* is about the life we amass while waiting for change.

Writing is hard graft, and this play was hard won. Like my characters, I had to exercise patience and fragility to get to the heart of the matter. I hope I have written a play about how to walk alongside unexpected loss and how help often comes from where you least expect it.

Any company that engages in the herculean and important task of creating new Australian work is a champion. I am very grateful for the trust, dramaturgy and spirit Canberra Youth Theatre invested in this project. This script is riddled with the smarts and funny bones of all the young people who contributed to its many drafts. Luke Rogers has been a generous ally during my writing process; his notes helped me see the wood for the trees while trying to unlock this story.

I grew up in the birthplace of this play and went to Canberra Youth Theatre; in so many respects, this work feels like a homecoming. I wish I could have told my sixteen-year-old self this would happen.

*Rosieville* is unashamedly sentimental in the true sense of the word. It is dedicated to my beloved friend Ken. He read it and told me it was good. I hope you think so too.

PS. All the pigeon facts in *Rosieville* are true. Who knew those rats of the sky were so amazing? Sometimes there is magic in the ordinary.

**Mary Rachel Brown**

I never thought I'd be making a work about pigeons.

*"The birds that come last are more incredible than the ones that win. They go way off course, make all sorts of wrong choices, yet they still manage to get home. Sometimes they are only one day behind the winning bird, but they have flown twice the distance."*

These lines go to the heart of what this story is about for me. Sometime it takes not coming first to understand what it is we truly value.

Each generation faces unique anxieties and challenges when it comes to understanding their future. In 2020, at the height of the pandemic, the word 'resilience' was being thrown around a lot. For young people, there was not only a sense of uncertainty, but the loss of something intangible. Time, connection, community, hope? It was a shit time.

I invited Mary to write a play for Canberra Youth Theatre that wrestled with the complexities of what young people were feeling amongst all of this chaos. How do we face the things that we're scared of? What does it feel like to encounter grief for the first time? How do we build a compassionate relationship with the difficulties we face, and accept what we can't control? There are major life events that can completely destabilise a young person's world. We need to share stories that reflec those experiences, and offer a message of hope and resilience.

In *Rosieville*, we encounter adults who are trying to do the best they can in the face of illness, relationships breakdowns, and catastrophic haircuts. We witness young people growing up, much faster than they'e like to, in order to fill the gaps around them.

*Rosieville* is a heartfelt work about family, community, perseverance, and helping each other through the big, world-shattering changes that life throws at us. Some of the most poignant moments for me in this play are the ones where the child needs to become the carer; to rise up and nurture. Bringing adult actors together with young performers allows us to paint a sensitive portrait of intergenerational connections, with an emphasis on the perspective of youth.

And yes, this is a play about pigeons. They are loyal, determined, take-no-shit, and against the odds, always manage to find their way home. Sometimes it takes a pigeon to teach us how to get back up after gettin knocked down by a blow to the heart.

This touching story is also a homecoming of sorts for Mary Rachel Brown, who participated with Canberra Youth Theatre as a teenager, and now as a multi-award-winning playwright, has written a play that brings her work back home.

**Luke Rogers**

## MARY RACHEL BROWN | PLAYWRIGHT

Mary Rachel Brown is a proud alumni of Canberra Youth Theatre, it was a big highlight in her crazy gothic youth, so having her play produced by Canberra Youth Theatre is a thrill. Mary has an Associate Diploma in Performing Arts and is the recipient of the following National Playwriting Awards: the Lysicrates Prize, the Rodney Seaborn Award, the Max Afford Award, and the Griffin Award. Her latest work *Rosieville* was runner-up in the 2021 Shane and Cathryn Brennan Prize. Mary's most notable work is *The Dapto Chaser*, which was commissioned and developed by Merrigong and reproduced by Apocalypse Theatre. The play was screened at Dendy Cinemas as part of Australian Theatre Live's program. Other works for the stage include *Betty Blokk Buster Reimagined* (Sydney Festival – contributing writer), *Dead Cat Bounce* (Griffin Theatre Company), *All My Sleep and Waking* (Apocalypse Theatre), *Permission to Spin* (Apocalypse Theatre), *Inside Out* (Christine Dunstan Productions), and an adaptation of *Die Fledermaus* (Sydney Conservatorium of Music). Mary's TV credits include sketch writing for *The Elegant Gentleman's Guide to Knife Fighting* for ABC and several episodes of *Home and Away* for Channel 7. Mary is a proud member of the Australian Writers Guild and supporter of WITS (Women in Theatre and Screen).

## LUKE ROGERS | DIRECTOR

Luke Rogers is the Artistic Director & CEO of Canberra Yout Theatre. He is a graduate of NIDA (Directing) and Theatr Nepean (Acting), and the Artistic Director of Stories Lik These. Luke is currently completing a Masters of Fine Arts i Cultural Leadership at NIDA. Previous roles include Theatr Manager of New Theatre, Artistic Director of The Spar Room, and Resident Studio Artist at Griffin Theatre Compan Directing credits include: *Collected Stories* (Chaika Theatre ACT Hub), *The Trials, How To Vote!, Dags, Two Twent Somethings Decide Never To Be Stressed About Anythin Ever Again Ever, Little Girls Alone in the Woods, Norma Possibility, Collapse* (Canberra Youth Theatre), *In Real Lif* (Darlinghurst Theatre Company), *Blink, MinusOneSiste Fireface, The Last Five Years, The Carnivores* (Stories Lik These), *Play House* (NIDA), *The Pillowman, Waiting For Godo Don Juan in Soho, Art is a Weapon, After The End, Blaste* (New Theatre), *100 Reasons For War, Love and Informatio Spring Awakening, A Midsummer Night's Dream, Shoot/G Treasure/Repeat, Shakespeare's Women* (AFTT), *Lysistrat The Burial At Thebes, Pool (No Water), 4.48 Psychosis, Eye To The Floor* (Sydney Theatre School), *A Midsummer Night Dream, Mr Marmalade* (CQUniversity), *Macbeth, Cyberbil Embers* (AIM Dramatic Arts), and *Two Weeks With The Quee* (Mountains Youth Theatre). Tour Director: *The Witche* (Griffin). Assistant Director: *Eight Gigabytes of Hardcor Pornography* (Griffin/Perth Theatre Company), *Story of th Red Mountains* (NIDA), The Boys (Griffin/Sydney Festival *Steel Magnolias* (Blackbird Productions), *Assassins* and *Th Crucible* (New Theatre). Luke regularly directs and lecture at various universities and drama schools. He was a membe of Directors Lab: Melbourne (Theatre Works/Melbourn Festival), and Playwriting Australia's Dramaturgy Progra and Directors Studio.

## EMILY AUSTIN | ASSISTANT DIRECTOR

Emily Austin is an emerging director and theatre-mak from Melbourne. She is in her fourth year of study, current completing a Bachelor of Arts/Laws (Hon) at ANU. Emi has being involved in many productions, including directin *When the Rain Stops Falling* (2022), various crew roles in *Th Laramie Project* (2022), *Catch-22* (2022), *Arcadia* (2021 and assistant directing *The Trials* (2023). She is currently th Artistic Director of the National University Theatre Societ and is working to curate and produce their season, focuse on providing new opportunities for students within the art Emily is very excited to develop her skills as a Resident Artis at Canberra Youth Theatre.

## AISLINN KING | SET & COSTUME DESIGNER

Aislinn is drawn to creating immersive experiences inspired by movement, gesture, light and material exploration. Graduating from NIDA with a Master of Fine Arts Design for Performance, Aislinn was awarded the MADE by the Opera House scholarship to Denmark in 2020 and was selected to exhibit at World Stage Design 2022 in Calgary, Canada, supported by an artsACT grant. In 2022, Aislinn also received the Australian Production Design Guild APDG Emerging Designer for Live Performance Award for the design of Canberra Youth Theatre's production of *Two Twenty Somethings Decide Never To Be Stressed About Anything Ever Again. Ever.* Aislinn has been a designer on four Canberra Youth Theatre productions, including *Little Girls Alone in the Woods* (2021), *Two Twenty Somethings...* (2021), *Dags* (2022), and *Rosieville* (2023). The design for *Rosieville* sets up a gradient of tones and intensities. The materiality of the set holds both rawness and brightness in an interchange of thresholds, implied and imagined. An overlay of whimsy is drawn across the design elements, expressed in exaggerations of scale and a few unwarranted pigeon splats.

## ETHAN HAMILL | LIGHTING DESIGNER

Ethan Hamill is an emerging live event and theatre practitioner, who specialises in lighting, video design and programming/systems. In 2023, Ethan graduated from the National Institute of Dramatic Art (NIDA) with a Bachelor of Fine Arts in Technical Theatre and Stage Management. He is a Resident Artist for Canberra Youth Theatre in 2023, whilst also working across Sydney's theatre and live event scene. Ethan strives to keep up with new and emerging technologies, and is always trying to incorporate these into his work. Ethan's recent credits include: lighting programmer for *Is God Is* (Sydney Theatre Company, 2023), and *The Dismissal: An Extremely Serious Musical Comedy* (Squabbalogic, 2023), lighting designer for *You Can't Tell Anyone* and *The Trials* (Canberra Youth Theatre, 2023), lighting operator for *Do Not Go Gentle* (Sydney Theatre Company, 2023), swing lighting operator for *Joseph and the Amazing Technicolour Dreamcoat* (Sydney season, 2023), lighting designer for *The Magic Flute* (NIDA, 2022), video designer for *How to Vote!* (Canberra Youth Theatre, 2022), production manager for *Falsettos* (NIDA, 2022), and co-video designer for *Eat Me* (STC/NIDA Collaboration, 2021).

# CREATIVE TEAM

## PATRICK HAESLER |
## SOUND DESIGNER & COMPOSER

Patrick Haesler is a composer, performer, sound designer and recording artist from Canberra, Australia (Ngunnawal Country). Beginning as a trumpet player, Patrick has since branched into numerous musical fields, drawing influences from jazz and progressive music. In 2018 Patrick entered the world of theatre, acting as musical director for ANU's Arts Revue. Since then, he has reprised this role as well as composing music and designing sound for several theatre productions. These include *The Initiation* (2022), *How To Vote!* (2022), *Soul Trading* (2022 & 2023), *The Trials* (2023) and *You Can't Tell Anyone* (2023). Patrick has released soundtrack albums for many of these productions. Most recently, in July 2023 Patrick released the soundtrack for *How to Vote!*, a 23-track album featuring music from and inspired by the play. The album contains music in a range of styles to complement the play's blending of student drama and political thriller. Patrick's experience with a wide variety of musical genres, ensembles and production techniques have made him a versatile creative in the world of music and sound. He is a Resident Artist at Canberra Youth Theatre for 2023.

## RHILEY WINNETT | STAGE MANAGER

Rhiley Winnett is a passionate, emerging stage manager, dedicated to working with young people and giving them the respect and opportunities that they may not be presented with otherwise. Rhiley has worked as stage manager on nine shows with Canberra Youth Theatre over the last few years including: *Normal* (2020), *Little Girls Alone in the Woods* (2021), *Two Twenty Somethings Decide Never To Be Stressed About Anything Ever Again. Ever.* (2021), *Dags* (2022), *The Initiation* (2022), *How to Vote!* (2022), *Soul Trading* (2022), *The Trials* (2023) and *You Can't Tell Anyone* (2023). Rhiley was thrilled to be offered the opportunity to continue working with Canberra Youth Theatre as stage manager for their 2023 shows, and as part of their 2023 Resident Artist program.

## OSCAR ABRAHAM | XAVIER

Oscar Abraham is excited to play Xavier in *Rosieville* in his first production with Canberra Youth Theatre. Oscar has taken theatre and improvisation classes since he was 7 years old and has been a regular workshop participant at Canberra Youth Theatre since 2020. Outside of theatre, Oscar loves public speaking, debating competitions and playing the piano. He also has a soft spot for his cocker-spaniel puppy named Hedy Lamarr.

## IMOGEN BIGSBY-CHAMBERLIN | ROSE

Imogen Bigsby-Chamberlin has been involved with Canberra Youth Theatre for seven years. Her production credits include *Little Girls Alone in the Woods* (2021), *Soul Trading* (2022), and most recently, *The Trials* (2023). She is beyond excited to be playing Rose because she has a very complex way of thinking which she hopes to show while performing. Outside of theatre, she plays basketball and the drums.

## AMY CRAWFORD | LIZ

Amy Crawford is a seasoned improviser and actor in the Canberra region. She regularly performs with the Canberra Repertory Society, with credits including *Our Country's Good* as Captain Arthur Phillip and John Wisehammer (2022), in the Ensemble for *A Christmas Carol* (2021), and *Brighton Beach Memoirs* as Blanche (2020). Amy won best actor in Canberra's Short+Sweet Festival (2019). In 2016, Amy co-founded Lightbulb Improv, an improvised theatre company that performs monthly comedy shows and festivals (Canberra Comedy Festival; New Zealand Improv Festival) and genre comedies (*The Family Business*, *Shakespeare: Off the Ruff* and *Under the Bonnet*). Amy has taught, performed and directed a range of improvised formats, including long-form dramas and musicals.

# CAST

## CALLUM DOHERTY | BEN

Callum Doherty is a multi-award losing actor with over ten years experience. He was recently the Assistant Director of *Puffs* and *God of Carnage* (Echo Theatre). Select performance credits include Stew in *How to Vote!* (Canberra Youth Theatre), Alva in *This Changes Everything* (Echo Theatre), Charlie in *Jasper Jones* (Budding Theatre), Nathan in *The Full Monty* (SUPA Productions), Luke in *Strictly Ballroom* (Canberra Philharmonic Society), Pugsley in *The Addams Family* (The Q), Winthrop in *The Music Man* (Queanbeyan Players), and Michael in *Mary Poppins* (Free Rain Theatre). Callum has also performed with the Canberra Comedy Festival and currently the Starlight Children's Foundation.

## CLAIRE IMLACH | PIGEON / CINDY

Claire Imlach is delighted to bring the roles of Pigeon and Cindy to the stage. When she is not playing a rat with wings, Claire enjoys drinking copious amounts of bubble tea and knitting up a storm (like the old lady she is). She is currently in her fourth and final year of her Bachelor of Education (Early Childhood and Primary) degree. She is looking forward to bringing drama and the arts to a new generation of primary students. Claire joined the Canberra Youth Theatre community in 2021. Since then, she has been a member of Emerge Company in 2021 and 2022, and the cast of *How to Vote!* Coo Coo!

## RICHARD MANNING | ALAN

Richard Manning has done various bits and bobs of a creative nature over the past few (lots of) years. He has played guitar in various bands – from rocky persuasions to jazzy persuasions – as well as The Blamey Street Big Band for quite a few years. He has sat understage, again with his guitar, in a number of musicals such as *Cats* (ANU), *Spring Awakening* (Phoenix Players) *Godspell* and *Hello Dolly* (Queanbeyan Players). Richard has also been a drama teacher at Canberra high schools and colleges, and directed Year 10 and Year 12 students in plays as diverse as *Royal Hunt of the Sun*, *A Clockwork Orange*, *Blackrock*, *The Golden Age,* and *Dust*. Since retiring, he has performed above stage, recently as Capulet in *Romeo and Juliet* for Canberra REP, as Ray in *Ruben Guthrie* for Wander Theatre and now as Alan in *Rosieville* for Canberra Youth Theatre. Now let's also talk about golf...!

## DISA SWIFTE | ANIKA

Disa Swifte is a theatre-maker and actor who has been involved in theatre since 2021, beginning with Canberra Youth Theatre's *Little Girls Alone in the Woods*. Over the past two years, Disa has gained experience in acting, directing, writing, stage management, and various behind the scenes roles. This year, Disa played the role of Sye in Sunny Productions' *Happy Meals Happy Kids,* and began acting in short films with their role of Little Sister in Sunspot Cinematic's *Halo*. Disa was a member of Canberra Youth Theatre's 2023 Emerge Company, where they developed and performed in the original production of *Sympathetic Resonance*. This is Disa's fifth production with Canberra Youth Theatre and they hope to continue to work with them in the coming years.

# OUR PARTNERS

We gratefully acknowledge the generous support of our partners who are key to the success of our work.

## GOVERNMENT PARTNER

Supported by

## CREATIVE PARTNERS

Ainslie and Gorman
Arts Centres

CANBERRA
**THEATRE**
CENTRE

## PROGRAM PARTNERS

HOLDING REDLICH

*ActewAGL*

## PRODUCTION SPONSORS

Sidestage

ELECT PRINTING

## MAJOR DONORS

THE
JEREMY SPENCER BROOM
LEGACY

## PRODUCERS CIRCLE

MICHAEL ADENA & JOANNE DALY
AMY CRAWFORD
PAUL & SHOBNA GOODING
MELINDA HILLERY

PETER & CASSANDRA HOOLIHAN
PETER & JANELLE MACGINLEY
TRACY NOBLE
RIDEAUX & FANNING FAMILY

CHRIS & ZOE WAGNER
ANONYMOUS (3)
as of August 2023

If you would like to know more about how you can support us, or are interested in partnering with us, contact **luke@canberrayouththeatre.com.au**

# CANBERRA YOUTHTHEATRE

## STAFF

**ARTISTIC DIRECTOR & CEO**
LUKE ROGERS

**ADMINISTRATOR**
HELEN WOJTAS

**FINANCE & STRATEGY MANAGER**
LOUISE DAVIDSON

**MARKETING & ENGAGEMENT MANAGER**
CHRISTOPHER CARROLL

**WORKSHOPS MANAGER**
BETH AVERY

**MARKETING & WORKSHOPS COORDINATOR**
LACHLAN HOUEN

## RESIDENT ARTISTS

EMILY AUSTIN          PATRICK HAESLER
ETHAN HAMILL          AISLINN KING
RHILEY WINNETT

## COMMISSIONED WRITERS

HONOR WEBSTER-MANNISON

## BOARD

PETER HOOLIHAN (CHAIR)
ADRIANA LAW (DEPUTY CHAIR)
CASSANDRA HOOLIHAN (SECRETARY)
ELLEN HARVEY (TREASURER)
AMY CRAWFORD
JOANNA ERSKINE
MEL ZIARNO

## WORKSHOP ARTISTS

CAITLIN BAKER
ELLA BUCKLEY
ASHLEIGH BUTLER
ELLIOT CLEAVES
REBECCA DUKE
QUINN GOODWIN
ANNA JOHNSTONE
CHARLIE LEHMANN
RACHEL ROBERTSON

GORMAN ARTS CENTRE
BATMAN STREET BRADDON ACT 2612
02 6248 5057
INFO@CANBERRAYOUTHTHEATRE.COM.AU

## CANBERRAYOUTHTHEATRE.COM.AU

@canberrayouththeatre

www.ingramcontent.com/pod-product-compliance
Lightning Source LLC
Chambersburg PA
CBHW050025090426
42734CB00021B/3430